Written and compiled by Peter Eldin
Illustrated by William Rudling

HENDERSON
PUBLISHING PLC

Magic Skills

Most people think that the way a trick works is the most important part of conjuring.
This is not true.

Magicians use lots of different skills to fool and entertain audiences.

All of the tricks in this book will help you develop those skills.

CO-ORDINATION
Co-ordination is needed by a magician for there are many tricks where you will appear to be doing one thing but you will really be doing something else.

MISDIRECTION
Misdirection is the art of distracting the spectators' attention away from something you do not wish them to know about.

Go Coin

This trick will help you develop the skills of co-ordination and misdirection. As with all tricks you must practise this in secret until you can do it perfectly.

Place a coin on your left palm, near to the base of the thumb. Put another coin on the right hand at the bottom of the first two fingers. The position of the coins is important.

Rest your hands, palm upwards, on a table. Now quickly turn both hands over and towards each other at the same time.

As soon as the hands are palm down, move them apart. All these actions should blend smoothly together into one continuous movement.

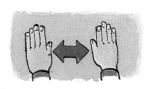

Now turn your hands over again. Everyone will expect to see a coin beneath each hand but both are now under the left hand!

It looks like difficult *sleight of hand* but the whole secret is in the position of the coins at the start. When you turn the hands over quickly the coin from the right hand is thrown across to the left.

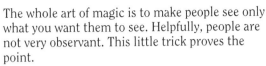

The whole art of magic is to make people see only what you want them to see. Helpfully, people are not very observant. This little trick proves the point.

Take three glasses or cups and place them on the table as shown in the first picture. You now have three moves to turn the glasses over so they are all right side up. To do this you must turn two glasses over at a time.

This is what you do:
Turn over glasses 2 and 3.

Cross your arms, pick up glasses 1 and 3, and turn them over.

For the third move, turn over glasses 2 and 3 again. All the glasses are now mouth upwards.

It seems simple enough to do so you now turn the middle glass upside down and challenge someone else to have a go.

Even if they've followed your moves exactly they won't be able to do it.

Why? Because the glasses are not in exactly the same position as they were at the start. You start with glasses 1 and 3 upside down but the spectator starts with 1 and 3 the right way up and only glass 2 is upside down.

It is impossible to do the trick from this position but people do not notice that it is different from the starting position you used.

This trick helps you develop your skills of co-ordination and misdirection. The secret relies on you being able to do two things - one secret - at the same time. To misdirect people's attention you have to be looking at and talking to the spectators - so there is quite a lot to practise.

Secretly stick a coin (using Plasticine or soap) under the edge of your table top.

Start the trick by placing four coins on the table. Make sure the audience can see that your hands are empty. Don't say "My hands are empty." That will make everyone aware you are about to do something. Simply talk and move your hands naturally. You could say, "Watch" and hold up both hands.

Point to the coins and count them. Scoop them onto your left hand, all the time concentrating on your audience. At the same time your left hand goes under the table top and pulls off the hidden coin. You must practise until you can do this naturally and without thinking about it.

Hold up your hand and ask how many coins it contains. When someone says "Four", open your hand and allow the five coins to fall onto the table.

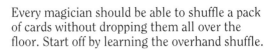

● Every magician should be able to shuffle a pack of cards without dropping them all over the floor. Start off by learning the overhand shuffle.

● Hold the pack in your right hand with the thumb at one end of the pack and the first three fingers at the other end. The little finger goes under the pack to keep all the cards neatly together.

Place your left hand, palm upwards, just below the pack. The pack should be tilted to an angle of about 45 degrees.

Press your left thumb against the top card. Now lift the right hand and a few cards will be pulled from the top of the pack to drop onto the left fingers.

● Bring the right hand back to the left again and repeat the movement so that another batch of cards falls onto those already in the left hand.

● Keep repeating these actions until all the cards are in your left hand. Practise your shuffling until you can do it quickly and smoothly.

The Riffle Shuffle

This looks impressive and shuffles the cards well.

1. Hold the pack upright in your right hand. The bottom of the cards rest on your fingers and your thumb is on top of the cards. Bend your forefinger and press it against the top card.

2. Your thumb now cuts the pack in two; half the cards fall onto your left hand.

3. Lift the end of the left packet with right second finger tip; hold in place with left thumb.

4. The two packets should now be face to face and held in the same position by each hand.

5. Lower the hands so that the thumbs come together, back to back. Bend the cards between your thumbs and fingers (your forefingers pushing against the back of each packet).

6. Let your thumbs release the cards, one by one, so that they become interleaved. This is easier to do if the backs of your fingers are resting on a table so that the cards drop onto the table.

7. Now push the two halves of the pack together and the shuffle is complete.

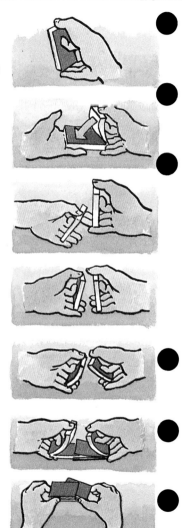

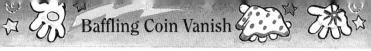

It is not only the magician who has to develop his or her skills. The assistant is also an important part of the act. In some tricks, as in this one, the audience must not know that an assistant is being used.

Show a coin on the palm of your hand and then cover it with a handkerchief. Go to each of your friends in turn and allow them to feel under the handkerchief to make sure the coin is still there. Then you whisk the handkerchief off your hand and the coin has vanished!

The trick appears to be done by accomplished sleight of hand but, in fact, the last person to feel beneath the handkerchief is your secret accomplice. He or she simply takes the coin from your hand. This must be done carefully so that no-one else guesses what has happened. Wave your free hand over the handkerchief in a mysterious manner and whisk the handkerchief away to show that the coin has disappeared.

Sleight of Hand

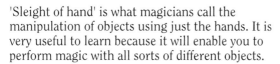

'Sleight of hand' is what magicians call the manipulation of objects using just the hands. It is very useful to learn because it will enable you to perform magic with all sorts of different objects.

The French Drop

This sleight is useful for vanishing coins and other small objects.

1. Hold a coin between the first finger and thumb of your left hand.

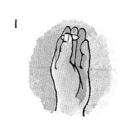

I

2. The right hand now approaches the left and goes around the coin.

2

3-4. Close the right hand as if taking the coin but then secretly allow the coin to drop into your left hand.

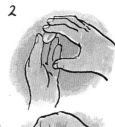

5. Move your right hand away as if it holds the coin.

3

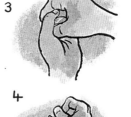

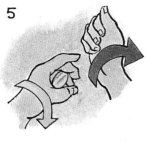

5

4

6. The coin actually remains hidden in your left hand. Try to forget about this and hold your left hand naturally. As the right hand moves away allow your left hand to drop to your side.

Keep looking at the right hand while you are doing this. This is important. If you look at your right hand, your spectators will look at it as well. This helps convince everyone that the coin really is in that hand and draws attention away from the left hand.

8. Pretend to throw the coin from your right hand into the air. Watch its invisible flight as it goes into the air - the coin has vanished!

THE MAGICIAN AS AN ACTOR
One of the most important skills that a magician must have is the ability to act. You have to act like a real magician to make your tricks more impressive. The easiest way to do this is to pretend that you really do have magical powers.

Often in card tricks it is necessary to control a chosen card to the top of the pack whilst apparently shuffling the cards quite fairly. Here is a relatively simple method.

1. Have a card selected. Hold the pack in your left hand. With your right hand, lift off the top half of the pack.

2. Ask the spectator to drop the chosen card on top of the lower part of the pack.

3. Return the top half of the pack onto the bottom half.

4. In doing this, however, drop the top half a little forward to the bottom half. This creates what magicians call a 'step' in the pack.

5. Bring the right hand back to the pack and lift off the top half. The step in the pack makes this very easy to do.

6. Swivel your left hand so the bottom card is facing the audience.

7. Now shuffle off the top half of the pack, face up, onto the lower half. It looks like a perfectly fair procedure but the top card of the pack is now the chosen card.

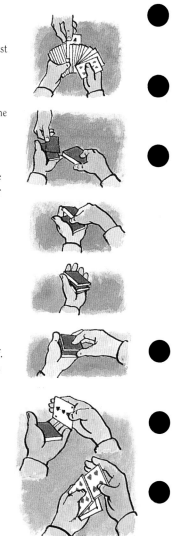

It is useful in card tricks to be able to cut the cards without actually changing the order. Magicians call this a false cut. Here's one to try:

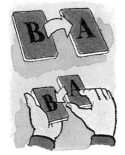

Place the pack on the table a short way from you. Lift off about half the pack (A) and place it down on the table near to you.

With your right hand pick up the remaining cards (B) and put them in your left hand.

Now pick up A and place it on top of the cards in your left hand. If you do this casually, it appears quite normal. In fact the cards are still in the same order as they were when you started!

MAGIC TIP

When you try this for the first time you may not believe anyone will be fooled - it's too simple. In fact, some of the most effective magic is surprisingly simple. The secret is in being completely natural. Just cut the cards as described, without making any comment, and people will accept it as a proper cutting of the cards.

Here is a more spectacular way to secretly get a card to the top of the pack. It's reasonably easy but you must practise until it comes naturally.

1. The cards are shuffled and spread face down for someone to take one. Square up the pack as the card is shown to everyone else.

2. Lift off the top half of the pack and ask the spectator to put their card face down on top of the lower half.

3. Drop the upper portion back on top so the card is 'lost' in the pack. What actually happens is that you secretly put the tip of your left little finger on top of the chosen card just before you drop the rest of the cards on top.

From the front, the pack looks quite ordinary but at your end there is a gap (magicians call this a 'break') caused by your left fingertip.

Now say: "I'll just give the pack a double turnover cut so your card is completely lost." Turn your left hand so all the cards above your little finger fall face up onto your right hand.

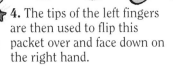

4. The tips of the left fingers are then used to flip this packet over and face down on the right hand.

5. Immediately this happens the left thumb and fingers are used to turn the packet in the left hand over and face up on the right hand alongside the face down first packet.

6. The left fingertips then turn this packet over and face down on top of the face down packet in the right hand.

The pack is now complete once again. It looks just like a clever flourish but in fact what the spectators do not know is that the chosen card is now on top of the pack.

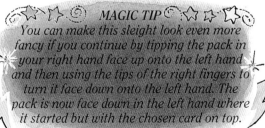

MAGIC TIP

You can make this sleight look even more fancy if you continue by tipping the pack in your right hand face up onto the left hand and then using the tips of the right fingers to turn it face down onto the left hand. The pack is now face down in the left hand where it started but with the chosen card on top.

A magician must possess acting ability. You don't just do the tricks, you must do them as if they were real magic. Here is a trick that relies upon your ability to act to make it convincing.

The cards are shuffled and a spectator is asked to remove any nine cards and place them face up on the table (as shown).

You go out of the room while someone chooses any one of the nine cards by pointing at it.

When you return to the room you tell everyone which card was chosen.

What the audience do not know is that one of them is your secret accomplice and that the pair of you have rehearsed this trick in private before showing it to anyone. The way the cards are placed on the table means that your secret assistant can signal to you which is the chosen card in a very subtle way.

You both imagine the face card of the pack to be divided into nine squares, representing the positions of the nine cards on the table.

Your secret assistant is the person who dealt out the cards at the start and still holds the pack when you come back into the room. All they have to do is hold the pack so that their thumb is in the same position as the chosen card.

When you come into the room a quick glance at your assistant's hand tells you all you need to know.

Do not make it obvious that you have looked at your friend or you will give the game away. You must now act like a real mind-reader, pretend to concentrate the power of your mind, and then name the card that was selected.

Ace Assembly

All magicians need to be able to do a false shuffle. The pack of cards is apparently shuffled quite fairly, but the magician keeps a certain card, or a number of cards, in the same position. One of the simplest keeps a number of cards on the top of the pack.

Place the four aces face down on top of the pack. Now do a riffle shuffle but allow the top four cards to remain on the top. In other words you riffle the two halves together as normal but the last four cards are allowed to fall all at once. The shuffle appears to be perfectly fair but the four aces remain on the top of the pack.

You can use this shuffle in a trick. Before your show, put the four aces on top of the pack and put the pack in its case. When you perform the trick you remove the pack from its case and do the false riffle shuffle.

Put the cards on the table and ask a spectator to cut off about three-quarters of the cards and pile them to the right. Now ask them to cut off about two-thirds of the cards from the larger pile and place them to the right. Finally ask them to cut the right pile in half and place those to the right. There will now be four piles of cards on the table. Only you know that the four aces are on the top of the right hand pile.

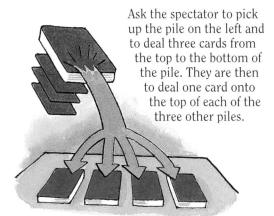

Ask the spectator to pick up the pile on the left and to deal three cards from the top to the bottom of the pile. They are then to deal one card onto the top of each of the three other piles.

Then ask them to do the same with the second pile, and the third and fourth piles.

Now wave your hands over the cards in a mysterious manner and ask the spectator to turn over the top card of each pile - they are the four aces! Seems impossible, but apart from the false shuffle at the beginning, it works itself.

Thumb Amputation

A magician should always be aware of 'angles'. It is possible to give away the secrets of some tricks if you aren't careful how they are presented to an audience. It is also important to be aware of what the audience sees, so you can display objects clearly.

In this trick the angle of presentation is so important that it is a good idea to try it out in front of a mirror before showing it to anyone.

It appears that you break your thumb in half and then restore it again. Don't worry - it is not as frightening as it sounds!

Hold your left hand up in front of you. The palm should be towards your body and the fingers pointing to the right.

Bend your left thumb in towards yourself. Now bend your other and place it against the left.

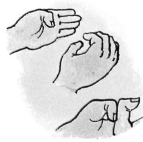

Your right forefinger should be placed in front of the thumbs where they touch. All the other right fingers should be held upwards so the thumb can be seen clearly.

If you look at this position in the mirror it should appear that you are showing just your left thumb.

Now move your right hand to the right and it appears that you have severed your thumb!

Move it back again to restore the thumb and then quickly open both hands.

Coin Go

1. For this trick you will need to 'prepare' a large handkerchief. Cut a corner from a matching handkerchief and sew it to the corner of the first to make a small bag, with a coin sewn in it.

2. You also need a matchbox containing another coin, and a marker pen which will write on coins. Put the box on a shelf or table away from your 'stage', and the handkerchief in your pocket.

3. To do the trick you first borrow a similar coin from someone. Ask them to mark the coin with the pen so they will recognise it later. While the coin is being marked, take the handkerchief from your pocket and drape it over your hand. Take the coin from the spectator and apparently wrap it in the handkerchief.

4. In fact you keep it hidden in your left hand as you bring the pocket-corner of the handkerchief to the centre.

5. Ask the lender of the coin to hold it through the handkerchief. Of course, it is the secret coin that they can feel.

6. Now say you are going to make the coin fly across the room. Take one corner of the handkerchief in your right hand and ask the spectator to let go. Give the handkerchief a shake and it seems that the coin has vanished.

Pretend to follow the imaginary flight of the coin across the room. While you are doing this casually put the handkerchief back in your pocket.

7. Now go to the matchbox. Make it easy to see that your right hand is empty as you use it to pick up the matchbox. Give the matchbox a shake and everyone will hear the coin inside.

8. Push the matchbox open to show someone the new coin inside. Pretend to tip the coin out onto your left hand. In fact, you hold the matchbox so the coin falls to the end of the drawer. Tip the box over onto your left hand.

9. Walk back across the room showing the borrowed coin on your left hand (where it has been hidden right from the start!). Hand the coin back to the spectator and ask them to confirm that it is their coin.

This trick is good for learning several skills. You have to keep the coin hidden in your hand. Believe that what you are doing is real magic; forget that the coin is in your hand. If you worry about it, you will transmit that worry to your audience and give the game away.

To follow the invisible flight of the coin across the room will need your acting skills - something that is very important in conjuring.

The fact that you show the coin in the box to someone takes a bit of nerve but you have to get used to this to be a good magician.

MAGIC TIP
The pocket in the handkerchief idea could also be used to make a borrowed ring vanish. Use a cheap brass ring inside the handkerchief, but get someone else to hold it as the owner may be able to feel that it is not their ring.